Air Fryer Cookbook

Amazingly Easy Recipes To Prepare (Bake, Grill, Roast, Quick and Easy, Low Oil, Simple, Clean Eating, Smart People, Delicious)

Sarah P. Williamson

If you find this book helpful, please leave a review on Amazon here. It will help others also find this book.

AF498106

Table of Contents

1 - Introduction

Thank you for purchasing the Air Fryer Cookbook! This cookbook is comprised of a delicious collection of recipes that are suitable for all tastes. Each recipe is simple to make, full of flavor, and offers a healthier alternative to traditionally fried foods. This book is made to help ensure you get the most out of your Air Fryer.

If you have yet to purchase an Air Fryer, you can get one at almost any kitchenware shop that sells small appliances. Or, if you are new to your Air Fryer, you may be wondering how it works! Air Fryers are a wonderful alternative to oil fryers. They cook the food by circulating hot air around it, similar to a convection oven. There is a mechanical fan inside that circulates the hot air at a high speed, which cooks the food and produces a delicious crispy outer layer, much like traditional fried food.

Thanks to its incredible abilities, Air Fryers are able to cook almost any fried food recipe with very little alteration. The outcome is always just as delicious, if not better, than its oil-fried counterpart. From dinner rolls to roasted meat, delicious snacks and sweet desserts, the Air Fryer can do just about anything your standard oven can do. Its wonderful range of abilities makes the Air Fryer even more valuable to a modern kitchen than a traditional oil-based fryer.

Throughout the pages of this book, you will discover a variety of sweet, savory, salty, citrusy, and other delicious recipes. These flavorful dishes are hand-picked to ensure you have a hearty collection of the best recipes on hand at all times. As a result, this cookbook is the ultimate companion book to any Air Fryer. You are guaranteed to find a wonderful selection of traditional, modern and alternative recipes inside to suit any palette. There is certainly something here for everyone.

2 - Appetizers

Blooming Onions

These fancy blooming onions are a tasty, gorgeous dish that is a wonderful addition to any meal. They taste similar to onion rings but have a beautifully different appeal. This recipe is easy, delicious, and crunchy.

Makes: 1 Onion, Can Serve 2-3 Portions If Shared.

Ingredients

- 1 large White Onion

- 1/4 cup Milk, nonfat

- 2 Eggs, large

- 3/4 of cup Panko Breadcrumbs

- 1 1/2 teaspoons Paprika

- 1 teaspoon Garlic Powder

- 1 teaspoon Salt

- 1/2 teaspoon Cajun Seasoning

- 1/2 teaspoon Black Pepper

Steps

1. Peel the onion, and cut the top off. Place the cut side down onto your cutting board. Starting around 1/2" from the root, slice the onion downward all the way to the cutting board. Repeat this process to make 4 evenly spaced cuts around the entire onion. Cut evenly between each section until you total 8 cuts.

2. Take a bowl of ice water, and soak the onion for at least 2 hours, but preferably overnight. When done soaking, remove the onion from the water and pat dry. Open each layer, so the "petals" are exposed.

3. In a bowl, mix panko breadcrumbs with olive oil and Cajun seasoning.

4. In a second bowl, mix salt & pepper.

5. In a third bowl, mix milk and egg.

6. Sprinkle the salt and pepper all over the onion, getting it in between all of the petals, then turn the

onion upside down to remove any excess.

7. Take a ladle and spoon the egg mixture all over the onion, making sure to get it in all of the crevices. Flip the onion upside down and let the extra egg mix drip off.

8. Generously coat the onion with bread crumb mixture, pressing it into place so it stays on.

9. Gently grease the Air Fryer basket and place the onion inside. Cover the top with aluminum foil, making a tent shape over the onion. Place the basket into the Air Fryer.

10. Cook the onion at 360F (182C) for 10 minutes.

11. Lift the foil to check the crispness of the onion. If it isn't done, replace the aluminum foil and cook for another 5-10 minutes to complete it.

12. When done, remove the onion carefully and serve with your choice of dressing. It pairs well with garlic aioli, ranch dressing or even blue cheese dressing.

Bread Sticks

These tasty bread sticks resemble those that you would order next to a pizza from any local pizza shop. They are light, fluffy, cheesy, and taste great dipped in any number of sauces from ranch dressing to marinara sauce.

Makes: 4 Servings

Ingredients

- Pizza Dough

- 4 3/4 cups Flour

- 1 (7g) pouch Instant Yeast

- 1 1/2 tablespoons Olive Oil

- 2 2/3 cup Warm Water

- 1/2 cup Warm Milk

- Dash of Salt

- Bread Sticks

- 1/3 of a Pizza Dough Recipe (see above and Step #1)

- 4 tablespoons Coconut Oil

- 2 tablespoons Desiccated Coconut

- 1 teaspoon Garlic Puree

- 1 teaspoon Parsley

- 1/4 cup Cheddar Cheese, grated

- Salt & Pepper to taste

- Bread Seeds (optional)

Steps

1. Preheat the Air Fryer to 356F (180C)

2. In a large mixing bowl, combine flour, yeast, and salt. Once it is well blended, stir in olive oil and warm milk. Gradually mix in the water, kneading it well until it forms a soft dough.

3. In a small pan, melt your coconut oil over low-medium heat. In a small bowl, combine your seasonings

and then add your melted coconut oil.

4. On a generously floured area of your counter, roll your pizza dough out until it resembles a rectangular shape about 3/4" thick. Brush it with your garlic oil mixture until it is evenly coated. Dust the top with desiccated coconut until you can no longer see the garlic, and then add a sprinkle of grated cheddar cheese. Finish off with a healthy sprinkle of bread seeds.

5. Cook the seasoned pizza dough in the Air Fryer for 10 minutes, then increase the temperature of the Air Fryer to 392F (200C) and cook for a further 5 minutes. The bread sticks are done when the outside has a nice crispy texture and the inside is free of any uncooked dough.

6. When done, remove from the bread from the Air Fryer, cut into fingers and serve hot.

Cauliflower Buffalo Bites

These delicious cauliflower buffalo bites are an incredible vegetarian alternative to buffalo chicken wings. Plus, if you omit the butter then the recipe becomes vegan! You don't have to be vegetarian or vegan to enjoy these incredible bites, though! They are crispy, flavor rich cauliflower bites are an incredible appetizer for anyone to enjoy. Plus, they take less than thirty minutes to make!

Makes: 2-4 Servings

Ingredients

- 1/8 teaspoon Pepper

- 1/4 teaspoon Salt

- 2 teaspoons Garlic Powder

- 1 tablespoon Butter, melted (use coconut oil for vegan alternative)

- 1/2 to 3/4 cup Buffalo Hot Sauce, adjust amount to adjust heat of your bites

- Olive Oil to drizzle

- 1 large Head Cauliflower

Steps

1. Preheat your Air Fryer to 450F (232C).

2. Cut your cauliflower into bite-sized florets, and place them in a 1 gallon sized Ziploc bag. Drizzle enough olive oil to just coat the cauliflower.

3. In the bag, add your salt, pepper, and garlic powder. Seal the bag and shake to mix your ingredients thoroughly and evenly cover all of the cauliflower florets.

4. Place in your Air Fryer and fry for about 15 minutes, checking them after about 10 minutes to make sure they don't get too soft. Your fork should enter with just a shade of resistance, to make sure they don't get soggy.

5. Remove the florets from your fryer and set aside. In a medium glass bowl, melt your butter and then add your hot sauce. Toss the cauliflower in the hot sauce mix and stir to evenly coat each bite.

6. Once coated, return them to the air fryer for about 5 minutes.

7. You can serve these with any dipping sauce you'd

like, such as Ranch salad dressing or Blue Cheese dip.

Notes

- To prevent your bites from being too spicy, start with only half the total amount of hot sauce in the recipe. That way you can add more if you desire.

Crab Sticks

These scrumptious, crispy and fragrant crab sticks are extremely simple to make. You can sprinkle them lightly with any seasonings you desire to make your preferred flavor. For this recipe, we will be making them Cajun flavored!

Makes: 2-3 Servings

Ingredients

- 2 teaspoons Sesame Oil, to toss

- 1 packet DODO Crab sticks

- Cajun Seasoning Powder (or any seasoning of your choice)

Steps

1. Preheat your Air Fryer to 320F (160C), for 5 minutes.

2. Start by breaking the DODO crab sticks in half, then shred them until they're in smaller pieces. Don't over-do the shredding, or they will become too small! The pieces should be roughly the same size so they cook evenly. You should end up with crab sticks that are about 1.5-2 cm width. If you want, instead you could unroll all of your crab sticks and cut them with a knife for a more uniform size.

3. In a bowl, lightly toss your crab sticks in the oil to cover them evenly.

4. Place them in the Air Fryer for 12 minutes or until they're golden brown. You don't need to lay them in a single layer, so you can feel free to just toss them in. Every few minutes, open the Air Fryer tray and use tongs to toss the crab sticks so that they cook evenly.

5. Once they are done, you can remove them from the Air Fryer and sprinkle them lightly with the Cajun seasoning or whichever seasoning you chose.

Fried Pickles

Who doesn't love pickles? Seriously, they go great with nearly anything: burgers, sandwiches, salads, on their own as snacks. You may have even heard of the local fair serving delicious fried pickles for one of their special dishes. Now, you don't have to wait all year for those tasty treats: you can make their healthier counterpart right in your own home!

Makes: 3-5 Servings

Ingredients

- 1/2 of teaspoon Paprika

- 1/2 of teaspoon Garlic Powder

- 1/2 of teaspoon Salt

- 1/4 of cup Milk

- 1/2 of cup Flour

- 1 Egg

- 1x 16oz. Jar of Dill Pickle Wedges

- For Spicy Ranch Dipping Sauce:

- 1/4 cup Ranch Dressing

- 1/4 cup Salsa (mild to spicy, your choice)

Steps

1. Preheat your Air Fryer to 450F (232C) for 5 minutes.

2. First, remove your pickles from the jar and dab them dry with a paper towel.

3. In a medium bowl, whisk together your milk and egg.

4. In a separate medium bowl, combine: paprika, garlic powder, salt and flour

5. Take your pickle wedges and dip them in the flour mix first, then the egg mix, then back into the flour mix for one final coating.

6. Carefully place each of the pickles into your fryer in a single layer. Cook the pickles for 5 minutes, until the outside is golden.

7. Transfer to a paper towel-lined cookie sheet to cool while you cook the next batch if you find it necessary to cook in batches.

8. While cooking, combine your ranch and salsa in a small bowl to create your dipping sauce.

9. Serve immediately.

Notes

- These fried pickle treats also go well with garlic dipping sauce, dill dipping sauce, roasted tomato dipping sauce or just about any other kind. Feel free to mix it up and try whatever you might enjoy!

Roasted Mushrooms

The tasty mixture of garlic and vermouth on these roasted mushrooms create a delicious, savory appetizer or side dish. They make a wonderful appetizer, side dish or even a topping on delicious burgers or mashed potatoes.

Makes: 2-4 Servings

Ingredients

- 2 tablespoons of White Vermouth (optional)

- 1 tablespoon Duck Fat

- 2 teaspoons Herbes De Provence

- 1/2 teaspoon Garlic Powder

- 2 pounds Mushrooms

Steps

1. You will want to wash your mushrooms before preparing them. Use a salad spinner to dry them, then cut them into quarters and set them aside.

2. In the pan of your paddle-type Air Fryer (such as an Actifry), heat the duck fat, garlic powder, and herbes de provence for 2 minutes. Use a wooden spoon to stir the ingredients to keep them from clumping. Once the mixture is heated, add the mushrooms and let them cook for 30 minutes. 5 minutes before they're done, add the white vermouth.

Notes

- These can be served steaming hot with grilled meats such as steak, meatloaf, etc.

- If you don't have access to herbes de provence, you can substitute with any combination of herbs you desire!

3 - Side Dishes

Baked Garlic Potatoes

These delightful baked potatoes make a wonderful side to any traditional dish such as steak, roast chicken, or casserole. They are a simple, flavorful twist on the classic baked potato dish.

Makes: 3 Baked Potatoes

Ingredients

- 3 medium Russet Baking Potatoes

- 2 tablespoons Olive Oil

- 1 tablespoon Garlic

- 1 tablespoon Salt

- 1 teaspoon Parsley

Steps

1. Preheat your Air Fryer to 392F (200C).

2. Rinse your potatoes, then pat dry. Using a fork, cre-

ate a few air holes in each potato.

3. Drizzle the olive oil over each of the potatoes. Once the potatoes are coated evenly, you can sprinkle the garlic, salt and parsley on the tops.

4. After you have coated your potatoes, place them in the basket of your Air Fryer and place the basket in the machine.

5. Cook your potatoes for 35-40 minutes, or until they're fork tender.

6. Once they're done, you can eat them as is, or top them with your favorite dressings, such as parsley and sour cream.

Dinner Rolls

What dish doesn't taste better with dinner rolls on the side? These buttery rolls are incredibly simple to throw together, and take almost no time to complete! They work perfect on the side of any dish, especially foods that can be spooned on top for added flavor, such as sloppy joes or pulled pork!

Makes: 22 Dinner Rolls

Ingredients

- 1/3 cup Sugar

- 4 cups Bread Flour

- 2 1/4 teaspoon Instant Yeast

- 1 1/2 teaspoon Salt

- 1/2 cup Butter + some extra for glaze

- 1 cup Milk, room temperature

- 2 Eggs

Steps

1. In your bread maker, assemble your ingredients in this exact order: milk, butter, sugar, eggs, salt, bread flour, yeast).

2. Select the "Dough" setting. Once the cycle is completed, remove the dough and turn it out onto a lightly floured surface. Punch the air out to eliminate

any air pockets in your rolls.

3. Once you have removed all of the air, divide your dough into 22 portions. Roll each portion into a ball. Line your Air Fryer basket with a baking sheet, and lightly grease the edges to prevent sticking, then place each ball into the basket in a single layer.

4. After all of the dough portions are layered in your Air Fryer basket, dampen a cloth and cover the basket to let the dough rise. It should take about 30 minutes for them to rise double in size.

5. When the dough is doubled in size, preheat your Air Fryer to 302F (150C). When hot, add the Air Fryer basket and bake your dinner rolls for about 13-15 minutes. The tops should be golden brown when they're done.

6. When your buns are done, and you've taken them out of the Air Fryer, lightly brush some melted butter on top of them to create a buttery glaze.

Notes

- For a darker golden color, you can bake your buns at 320F (160C) instead of 302F (150C), for roughly the same amount of time.

Eggplant Fries

Eggplant fries are an exciting twist on our favorite French fry recipe. They have a unique and light flavor, and pair well with anything you'd typically pair traditional French fries with.

Makes: 1-2 Servings

Ingredients

- 1 medium Eggplant

- 3 tablespoons Cornstarch

- 3 tablespoons Water

- 1 tablespoon Olive Oil

- A pinch of Salt

Steps

1. Start by preheating your Air Fryer to 390F (199C)

2. Cut your eggplant into two halves, and then slice each half into strips to make your fries.

3. In a bowl, toss your cornstarch, eggplant fries, olive oil and water.

4. Place your fries into the Air Fryer basket and cook for 20 minutes.

Notes

- To enhance the flavor of these Eggplant fries, try sprinkling the final product with some seasonings. Good ones to use would be: rosemary, dill, garlic, or thyme.

French Fries

What is a fryer if you can't make French fries? Air Fryers claim to make the best fries ever, even without oil, and we would have to agree. Naturally, we will include the recipe for you to replicate this amazing side dish for yourself.

Makes: 2-3 Servings

Ingredients

- 2 large Potatoes

- 1 tablespoon Olive Oil (can be replaced with 1 tablespoon Butter)

Steps

1. Wash and peel your potatoes, and cut them into the shape of French fries.

2. Fill a bowl with cold water, and let your fries soak for 30 minutes, then drain.

3. Preheat your air fryer to 320F (160C), when hot, put your fries in.

4. Immediately after you insert the fries, add your oil or butter and stir it in.

5. Cook your French fries for about 10-15 minutes, until they're golden in color.

Notes

- You can add an extra punch to these French fries by sprinkling the cooked fries with any mixture of seasonings you'd like. Our favorite is seasoning salt with touch of garlic powder.

Honey Roasted Carrots

Honey roasted carrots are a sweet, savory dish that complements almost any meat entrée. They are tender and filled with rich flavors that will entice your taste buds and enrich your dining experience.

Makes: 3-5 Servings

Ingredients

- 3 cups of Carrot Sticks, you can use baby carrots or cut your own

- 1 tablespoon Honey

- 1 tablespoon Olive Oil

- Salt and Pepper to taste.

Steps

1. Preheat your Air Fryer to 392F (200C).

2. In a medium bowl, combine carrots, honey and olive oil. Mix the ingredients together until the carrots coat evenly. Season the bowl with salt and pepper and mix again.

3. Cook the carrots in your Air Fryer for 12 minutes.

4. Serve hot, beside any of your favorite entrees.

Notes

- To further enhance the flavor impact, you can try adding extra seasonings such as rosemary, sage, basil, thyme, oregano or any combination of these. Experiment to see what you enjoy most!

Mac & Cheese

Mac and cheese is one of the best comfort foods. It can warm up a cold night or sum up a long, tiring day. Somewhere between the cheesy goodness and the filling noodles, there is a magical key that unlocks smiles for anyone who enjoys this dish.

Makes: 2-4 Servings

Ingredients

- 1/2 cup Broccoli or Cauliflower, cut into small, equal sized florets

- 1/2 cup Milk, warmed

- 1 1/2 cup Cheddar Cheese, grated

- 1 cup uncooked Macaroni Noodles

- 1 tablespoon Parmesan Cheese, grated

- Salt and Pepper to taste

Steps

1. On your stove, boil a pot of water over high heat. Once your water is boiling, reduce the temperature to medium heat, and stir in your macaroni noodles and vegetables. Simmer until the macaroni is al dente, and the vegetables are just fork tender, about 7-10 minutes. When it's done, drain and return them to the pot.

2. Heat your Air Fryer to 392F (200C)

3. Stir in milk and cheddar cheese, and toss to combine all of the ingredients in your pot. Sprinkle in your desired amount of salt and pepper.

4. Pour your macaroni into an oven safe dish, and sprinkle your grated parmesan cheese on top. Place the entire dish onto the Air Fryer basket and reduce the temperature of your Air Fryer to 356F (180C). Bake your macaroni for 15 minutes. Allow to sit for about 5-10 minutes in the Air Fryer before serving.

Notes

- Do not remove your pasta dish from the Air Fryer immediately, as your macaroni will be bubbling hot and it could result in burning yourself.

- You can add any types of vegetables you want when you're initially boiling the macaroni and vegetable mixture. Make sure whatever you're cooking is cut evenly into pieces that will cook in about the same amount of time the pasta will.

Onion Rings

These crispy onion rings make great side dishes, or can even be eaten as an appetizer on their own. You can serve them on family game night as a finger food, swap out French fries and use them instead in the traditional fish and chips meals, or even eat them with a homemade burger.

Makes: 2-4 Servings

Ingredients

- 1 1/4 cups of Flour

- 3/4 cups of Breadcrumbs, preferably Panko

- 1 teaspoon of Baking Powder

- 1 teaspoon of Salt

- 1 cup of Milk

- 1 Egg

- 1 large Onion, sliced into 1/4 inch rings

Steps

1. Preheat your Air Fryer to 360F (182C)

2. Separate your onion slices into individual rings.

3. In a small, clean mixing bowl combine: flour, salt, and baking powder. Dip each onion ring in your flour mixture until it is evenly coated.

4. With the remaining flour mixture, whisk in the egg and milk. Dip each floured onion ring back into the batter, and coat evenly.

5. In a shallow dish, spread out a layer of Panko breadcrumbs, and use it to evenly coat each onion ring until its completely covered in the breadcrumbs.

6. Place your onion rings in the Air Fryer basket, replace the basket into the Air Fryer, and cook for about 7-10 minutes. When they're golden brown and crispy, they are done. You can pop the tray open to check on how they're doing and shake them up a bit around 5 minutes in, to make sure they're cooking evenly.

Notes

- If you don't have Panko breadcrumbs on hand, you could use any other kind, or make your own fresh ones from 3 slices of bread.

Twice Fried Potatoes

Like twice baked potatoes, these mashed cheesy potatoes are just as amazing, if not better. They are creamy, and pair wonderfully with any entrée.

Makes: 2 Servings

Ingredients

- 1 medium Russet Potato

- 1/3 cup Sharp Cheddar Cheese, grated

- 2 tablespoons Heavy Cream

- 1 tablespoon Green Onion, finely chopped

- 1 tablespoon Unsalted Butter

- 1 teaspoon Olive Oil

- 1/4 teaspoon Salt

- 1/8 teaspoon Black Pepper, ground

- 2 strips Bacon, chopped into 1/2 inch pieces

Steps

1. Rub the potato with olive oil, and place in the basket of the Air Fryer. Close the drawer and cook the potato for 30 minutes at 400F (204C). When the timer stops, reset it for another 30 minutes and cook the potato until it is just fork tender. Remove it from the air fryer and let it cool for approximately 20 minutes.

2. While the potato finishes cooking, cook the bacon until crispy, about 10 minutes. Remove from heat and set it aside.

3. When the potato can be handled, slice it in half lengthwise and scoop out the center of the potato into a medium bowl. Leave about 1/4 inch boarder in the potato skin.

4. In the bowl with the potato, add bacon and bacon fat,

1/4 cup of the cheese, 1 1/2 teaspoon of green onions, heavy cream, butter, salt and pepper. Whisk it together until smooth, divide the mixture between the two potato skins and smooth out the surface using the back of a spoon. Sprinkle the two potatoes with the rest of the cheddar cheese, and place them side by side in the Air Fryer basket. Close the drawer, and cook for 20 minutes at 400F (204C), until the cheese melts and the tops are golden brown.

5. Remove the halves from the Air Fryer, and sprinkle the tops with the rest of the green onions. Serve hot, with any garnishing you'd like.

Vegetable Medley

This delicious medley combines the hearty flavors of zucchini, yellow squash, and carrots. It's a colorful dish that serves well next to any entrée.

Makes: 2-4 Servings

Ingredients

- 2 medium Carrots, washed, peeled and cut into 1"

cubes

- 1 medium Zucchini, trim off the ends, and cut it into 3/4" half moons

- 1 medium Yellow Squash, trim off the ends, and cut it into 3/4" half moons

- 1 tablespoon Tarragon Leaves, roughly chopped

- 1 teaspoon Salt

- 1/2 teaspoon Pepper, ground

- 6 teaspoons Olive Oil

Steps

1. In a small mixing bowl, combine carrots with olive oil and mix well. Place the carrots in the Air Fryer basket and close the drawer. Cook them for 5 minutes at 400F.

2. While the carrots are cooking, drizzle the remaining 4 teaspoons over the zucchini and yellow squash in a medium bowl. Toss well to coat them evenly, and add

them to the Air Fryer basket once the carrots are done. Cook the vegetables for 30 minutes, tossing them 2-3 times throughout, to ensure they cook evenly.

3. When the Air Fryer is done, remove the vegetables from the basket and toss them with tarragon. Serve them warm.

Wedge Fries

Wedge fries are an excellent side to any fried dish, such as fish and chips, chicken wings, or spicy drumsticks. These Paprika Wedge Fries are seasoned with a healthy coating of paprika and black pepper, to enhance their flavor and compliment any dish they are served next to.

Makes 3-5 Servings

Ingredients

- 4 medium Russet Potatoes

- 1 cup Olive Oil

- 1 cup Water

- 1 tablespoon Paprika

- 1/2 tablespoon Black Pepper

- A pinch of Salt

Steps

1. Scrub your potatoes clean to prevent any dirt from being baked on.

2. Boil a pot of water and cook your potatoes until they're just fork tender.

3. Once the potatoes are done, put them in your fridge to let them cool. This should take about 10 minutes.

4. When the potatoes are cool enough to be comfortably handled, take them out and cut them into wedges.

5. In a bowl, toss your wedges with olive oil, paprika, black pepper and salt.

6. Heat your Air Fryer to 390F (199C) and cook each batch for 10 minutes, giving the basket a good shake around the 5 minute mark to help them cook evenly.

Yam Potato Fries

Sweet potato fries are an incredible side dish, especially when served with a dipping sauce such as a garlic ranch infusion, or a chipotle mayo. As the name suggests, they are sweet, full of flavor and add a beautiful touch of color to any dish.

Makes: 2-4 Servings

Ingredients

- 2 medium Yam Potatoes

- 1 teaspoon Coconut Oil

Steps

1. Preheat your Air Fryer to 392F (200C)

2. Wash and peel your yam potatoes. Cut them into sticks.

3. In a medium bowl, melt your coconut oil in the microwave for about 10 seconds if it is solidified. Toss the potatoes in the coconut oil to evenly coat them.

4. Once the Air Fryer is hot, add your fries into the basket and cook them for about 9 minutes.

5. The fries are done when they're golden and crispy.

Notes

- These taste great dipped in garlic aioli, chipotle mayo, blue cheese dressing, or any other flavor-rich dressing.

Zucchini Fries

Another twist on classic French fries, the zucchini fries take our favorite squash and turn them into a flavorful and unique side dish. These pair wonderfully with roasted chicken, lamb, casseroles, or lasagna.

Makes: 3-5 Servings

Ingredients

- 4 medium Zucchini

- 3 tablespoons Cornstarch

- 3 tablespoons Water

- 1 tablespoon Olive Oil

- A dash of Salt

Steps

1. Preheat your Air Fryer to 390F (199C)

2. Cut your zucchini into fries by cutting them it half and then cutting each of the halves into strips.

3. In a bowl, combine: zucchini, olive oil, cornstarch and water. Toss to evenly coat the zucchini.

4. Place your zucchini fries into the Air Fryer basket and cook for 15 minutes. If 15 minutes is not enough, you can add an extra 5 minutes to achieve desired color and taste. The batter on the zucchini fries should come out golden brown in color.

4 - Entrees

Burgers

Burgers are a versatile meal that can be served in so many ways. With endless choices for toppings, seasonings, and bread choices, you can never go wrong with a good quality burger. Air Fryers can make excellent burger patties that are cooked to perfection. This recipe is an excellent alternative for anyone who doesn't have access to a barbecue, or for the off-season!

Makes: 4 Burger Patties

Ingredients

- 1/2-pound Lean Ground Beef

- 1 small Onion, diced

- 1 teaspoon Tomato sauce

- 1 teaspoon Mustard

- 1 teaspoon Basil

- 1 teaspoon Mixed Herbs (such as oregano, thyme,

marjoram, parsley, etc.)

- 1 clove Garlic, minced (or 1 teaspoon of minced garlic, garlic puree, etc.)

- Salt and Pepper to taste

- 1/4 cup Cheddar Cheese, shredded

- 4 Buns

- 1/2 cup Iceberg Lettuce, coarsely chopped

Steps

1. Preheat the Air Fryer to 392F (200C)

2. In a medium bowl, combine ground beef, onion, tomato sauce, mustard, basil, mixed herbs, garlic, and salt and pepper. Mix until well blended.

3. Form beef mixture into four burger patties, and place them in the Air Fryer cooking tray.

4. Cook the burger patties for 25 minutes

5. Reduce the Air Fryer temperature to 356F (180C),

and cook the burgers for another 20 minutes.

6. Serve on a bun topped with lettuce and cheese.

Notes

- For alternative flavors, instead of ground beef, you could use a mixed mince (which is pork and beef combined), lean ground pork, lean ground turkey, or lean ground chicken.

Cajun Salmon

This salmon dish is a wonderful addition to Chinese meals, but it can also be served on its own, or with a delicious side of fresh garden salad. It is rich with flavor, and an incredible way to enjoy a salmon dinner. This recipe serves one as an independent entrée or serves 2 if cut in half and served with an additional side.

Makes: 1-2 Servings

Ingredients

- 1-piece Salmon Fillet, fresh

- 1/2 tablespoon Cajun Seasoning

- A sprinkle of Sugar (optional)

- Juice of a quarter of a Lemon, for garnish

Steps

1. Preheat your Air Fryer to 356F (180C), for about 5 minutes.

2. Start by cleaning your salmon, and patting it dry with a clean paper towel. Over a plate, sprinkle your fillet with Cajun seasoning all over, make sure all sides are coated. Take care not to use too much seasoning. If you prefer to add a touch of sweetness to the flavor, sprinkle a light amount of sugar over each side.

3. If your fillet measures about 3/4" thick, Air Fry for 7 minutes. Make sure the salmon fillet is skin side up, using the grill pan. Squeeze your quarter of a lemon over the salmon, and serve immediately.

Notes

- You can eat this salmon as is, or garnish it with any

number of toppings, such as sour cream, tartar sauce, ranch dressing, etc.

Coconut Chicken Tenders

These delicious chicken tenders are covered with shredded coconut instead of breading. They pair wonderfully with a white lemon sauce or a chipotle mayo dip.

Ingredients

- 1-pound Chicken Tenders (about 8 pieces)

- 3/4 cup Shredded Coconut, sweetened

- 3/4 cup Panko Breadcrumbs

- 2 teaspoons Garlic Powder

- 1 teaspoon Salt

- 1/2 teaspoon Ground Black Pepper

- 2 large Eggs

- Cooking Spray

Steps

1. Preheat Air Fryer to 400F (204C). Spray the Air Fryer basket with cooking spray, and set aside.

2. Take a wide and shallow dish and combine: eggs, salt, garlic powder, and pepper. Mix until well combined. Using another wide and shallow dish, stir together the panko breadcrumbs and shredded coconut.

3. Take each chicken tender and dip it into the egg mixture, coating both sides. Let the excess drip off, then coat the egg with the coconut and bread crumb mixture. Once evenly coated, press the breading into the chicken to make sure it doesn't fall off during cooking. Then, place each chicken tender into the pre-greased Air Fry basket. Discard any excess egg and coconut mixture. Using the cooking spray, spray the tops of the chicken tenders until they're evenly covered.

4. Bake for 12-14 minutes. The chicken should be cooked through, and the coating is crisp and golden brown.

Dry Rub Chicken Wings

Chicken wings are a fun and tasty finger food that make a wonderful meal for game night. They are flavorful, filling, and go great with a side of fries or onion rings, which you can also make in your Air Fryer! (See appetizers & sides.)

Makes: 24 Chicken Wings

Ingredients

- 24 Chicken Wings

- 1/2 cup Brown Sugar

- 2 tablespoons Garlic Powder

- 2 tablespoons Salt (or to taste)

- 1 tablespoon Paprika

- 1 tablespoon Ground Cumin

- 1 tablespoon Mustard Powder

- 1 tablespoon Chili Powder

- 1 tablespoon Black Pepper

- 1 teaspoon Cayenne Pepper

- 1 cup Olive Oil

Steps

1. Preheat your Air Fryer to 400F (204C)

2. In a clean medium bowl, thoroughly combine brown sugar, garlic powder, salt, paprika, ground cumin, mustard powder, chili powder, black pepper and cayenne pepper.

3. Evenly coat each chicken wing with olive oil and place in baking sheet lined Air Fryer basket.

4. Using about half of the seasoning you have made, coat each chicken wing evenly.

5. Cook for 20 minutes in Air Fryer, and then sprinkle the remaining seasonings over top of the baking chicken.

6. Cook for another 15-25 minutes, or until your pre-

ferred texture is achieved, and the chicken is cooked through.

Notes

- If you have an empty seasoning shaker on hand, it can make the seasoning job a lot simpler. Plus, you can make extra and save it for future use!

Fish & Chips

Classic fish and chips are a wonderful dish for any occasion. The fish is crispy, fresh, rich with flavor, and pairs wonderfully with any of the French fry recipes we have in this book!

Makes: 4 Servings

Ingredients

- 2 Fish Fillets (catfish, cod, halibut, etc.)

- 1 1/2 cups of Panko breadcrumbs

- 1 medium Egg, beaten

- 1 Lemon: rind and juice

- 1 tablespoon Parsley

- Salt & Pepper to taste

Steps

1. Preheat your Air Fryer to 356F (180C)

2. Cut each fish fillet in half, so you have four hearty pieces of fish. Season each piece of fish with the juice of one lemon, and set aside for later.

3. In a medium mixing bowl, blend together: breadcrumbs, parsley, lemon rind, salt, and pepper. Evenly spread the mixture into a large baking tray.

4. Coat the fish with the beaten egg, and then dip it into the breadcrumbs to thoroughly cover it.

5. Cook your fish for 15 minutes, until it is nice and crispy. The aroma of the fish should fill your kitchen, to hint that it's done.

Notes

- Find the French fry recipes in the book to make with

this recipe! It pairs well with classic French fries or any of the alternatives we have featured in the sides and appetizers sections.

- If you prefer, you can use a batter on the fish, but this healthier alternative is equally as tasty.

French Toast Sticks

These quaint French toast sticks are a fun addition to any breakfast, or even on their own as a snack! They are easy-to-prepare finger food that delivers the traditional favorite of French toast in a fun new way.

Makes: 4 Servings

Ingredients

- 4 pieces of Bread, sliced to whatever thickness you desire

- 2 tablespoons of Butter, softened (or Margarine, if you prefer)

- 2 Eggs, lightly beaten

- Cinnamon

- Salt

- Nutmeg

- Cooking spray

- Icing Sugar, for garnish (optional)

- Maple Syrup, for garnish (optional)

Steps

1. Preheat your Air Fryer to 356F (180C)

2. In a medium mixing bowl, gently beat two eggs together. When the eggs are blended, add a heavy dash of cinnamon, a sprinkle of salt, and a small pinch of nutmeg.

3. Take the bread and butter both sides of each slice, then cut into 1" strips.

4. Dip each strip of toast in the egg mixture and coat them as evenly as possible. Arrange them in the Air

Fryer in a single layer. (This will require you to make two batches for the full recipe.)

5. Cook for 2 minutes, then pause the Air Fryer. Remove the pan and set it on a heat-safe surface. Using cooking spray, evenly spray the toast strips with cooking spray until they are completely covered.

6. After generously coating the French toast strips, turn them over and generously spray the other side as well.

7. Return the pan to the Air Fryer, bake for an additional 4 minutes. Make sure you check on the strips periodically to make sure they aren't burning. Check, too, that the strips are evenly cooking in the pan.

8. When the egg is thoroughly cooked, and the bread turns golden brown, you can remove your French toast sticks from the Air Fryer, garnish and serve them immediately

Notes

- If you wish to garnish your French toast, you could

use icing sugar, maple syrup, whip cream, or with a small bowl of fruit syrup on the side for dipping.

Fried Ravioli

This fried ravioli is healthy, tasty, and makes for a wonderful variation of regular ravioli. It is creamy, full of flavor, and delicious.

Makes: 2-4 Servings

Ingredients

- 1 small jar Marinara Sauce

- 1 medium box Cheese Ravioli (or Meat Ravioli)

- 2 cups Breadcrumbs

- 1 cup Buttermilk

- 1/4 cup Parmesan Cheese

- 1/2 tablespoon Olive Oil

Steps

1. Preheat the Air Fryer to 392F (200C)

2. Start by dipping the ravioli into buttermilk

3. In a medium bowl, mix the oil into breadcrumbs thoroughly. Then, press the ravioli into the bread-crumbs, until it is thoroughly coated.

4. Line the Air Fryer basket with parchment paper, and cook the breaded ravioli for about 5 minutes.

Fried Tofu

Tofu is a popular vegetarian alternative to meat products. It has a light, spongy texture that can develop a crispy exterior when cooked properly. It has a unique taste that suits nearly any dish, and can even be enjoyed on its own. Fried tofu is crispy, fresh, and full of delicious flavor.

Makes: 2-4 Servings

Ingredients

- A medium block of Firm Tofu (Organic, Non-GMO variety)

- 1/4 cup Rice Flour (can use Cornmeal as an alternative)

- 2 tablespoons Cornstarch

- 2 tablespoons Olive Oil

- 1/4 cup Parmesan Cheese, grated (optional)

- Salt & Pepper to taste

Steps

1. Drain your tofu, then slice it into 1" cubes. For the best outcome, you will want to dry your tofu. To do this: take two plates, some paper towel, and something that can be used as a weight. Line one of your plates with a paper towel, and then place all of the tofu on the paper towel with a little space between each, in one layer. Place another sheet of paper towel over the top of the tofu, and rest your second plate on top of the tofu. Rest a weight on the top plate to help encourage the drying process. Leave it for at least 30 minutes, but preferably a few hours, or as long as overnight.

2. When you're ready to cook, preheat your Air Fryer to 365F (185C)

3. In a medium mixing bowl, stir together cornstarch, rice flour, and cheese. Add your tofu cubes and mix them to coat them evenly.

4. Drizzle a little oil onto the tofu, and transfer it into the Air Fryer basket in your preheated fryer. Due to the amount, you will need to cook the tofu in batches. Do not overlap the tofu, it will prevent it from evenly cooking all the way through.

5. Cook for 7 minutes, then flip your tofu and cook it for another 7 minutes.

6. Sprinkle salt and pepper over the cooked tofu to taste, and serve.

Lemon Fish

Fish is highly known for its nutritional value. This citrusy dish features white fish that has been lightly flavored with lemon. It is an excellent alternative to the traditional fish and chips dish, and can be served with any side you desire:

we like it best with a fresh garden salad or zucchini fries.

Makes: 4 Pieces

Ingredients

- 2 pieces White Fish (any of your choice, i.e. cod, halibut, tilapia, etc.) cut to make 4 pieces

- 2 Lemons, juice one

- 1 1/2 cup Refined Flour, separated

- 1/2 cup + 3 tablespoons Water

- 1/4 cup Sugar

- 2 teaspoons Green Chili Sauce

- 1 teaspoon Red Chili Sauce

- 2 teaspoons Oil + enough to brush the tops of the fish

- 1 Egg White

- 4 teaspoons Corn Flour Slurry (1 teaspoon Corn Flour dissolved in 1 tablespoon Hot Water)

- 2-3 leaves Lettuce

- Salt to taste

Steps

1. Preheat your Air Fryer to 356F (180C)

2. In a medium mixing bowl, combine: 1 cup refined flour, salt, green chili sauce, oil, and egg white. Mix well, until it creates a thick batter.

3. Evenly spread out 1/2 cup refined flour on a plate.

4. Dip each fish fillet into the batter, then coat with refined flour. You may need to add more flour to the plate, depending on the size of your fillets.

5. Slice one of your lemons, and set it aside.

6. In a non-stick pan, boil 1/2 cup water. Once it's boiling, add sugar and stir constantly until the sugar dissolves.

7. Brush the Air Fryer basket with oil, place your fish fillets inside and cook for 15-20 minutes.

8. While that cooks, return to the syrup you have on the stove top. Add cornflour slurry and mix again, then add the red chili sauce. Mix well to combine all of the ingredients. Finally, add the lemon slices, and the juice of one of your lemons, and mix the sauce well. Cook until your sauce thickens. Do not cook on too high of a temperature, or you will burn your sauce.

9. Remove the fish from the Air Fryer basket, brush with oil, and return to the basket to cook for an additional 5 minutes.

10. Tear the lettuce leaves into large chunks and make a bed of lettuce on a serving platter. Place the fish on top of the lettuce, and top with the lemon sauce. Serve immediately.

Meatloaf

This meatloaf recipe is a wonderful recipe that works excellent in the Air Fryer. It takes approximately an hour and a half start to finish and satisfies any meatloaf cravings you may have.

Makes: 6-8 Servings

Ingredients

- 2 pounds Extra Lean Ground Beef

- 1 cup Panko Breadcrumbs

- 1/4 cup Onion, minced

- 1/4 cup Whole Milk

- 3 1/2 tablespoons Sour Cream

- 3 tablespoons Ketchup

- 1 1/2 tablespoons Worcestershire Sauce

- 1 tablespoon Butter

- 1 1/2 teaspoons Salt

- 1 1/2 teaspoons Black Pepper, freshly ground

- 2 cloves Garlic, minced

- 1 Egg, lightly beaten

- 1 (15 oz.) can Tomato Sauce, divided into two halves

Steps

1. Preheat your Air Fryer to 350F (177C)

2. In a skillet over medium heat, melt the butter. Once it is melted, sauté the onion and garlic for 5 minutes to tender the onions. Remove the onions from the heat, and season them with salt and pepper.

3. In a large mixing bowl, combine onion and garlic, beef, breadcrumbs, egg, Worcestershire sauce, sour cream, and 1/2 the tomato sauce. Gradually stir milk into the mix, 1 teaspoon at a time until the mixture is moist. Do not let the mix become soggy. Transfer the mixture you've created into the Air Fryer basket.

4. Bake the mix in the preheated Air Fryer for 40 minutes. Increase the temperature to 400F (204C), and bake for an additional 15 minutes until the internal temperature reaches 320F (160C).

5. In a small clean bowl, combine the remaining 1/2 of the tomato sauce and ketchup. Top your meatloaf with this mixture, and bake for a final 10 minutes.

Mini Basil & Broccoli Pizzas

Pizzas are timeless favorite, and these mini basil and broccoli pizzas are a perfect way to bring that classic to life in your Air Fryer! These pizzas can be customized to include any of your choice of toppings, but we love these ones and the way they bring a healthy spin to our favorite dish!

Makes: 4 Mini Pizzas

Ingredients

- The Dough

- 4 cups Flour

- 1 (7g) pack Instant Yeast

- 1 cup Tepid Water (2 parts cold, 1 part boiling)

- 2 tablespoons Extra Virgin Olive Oil

- The Toppings

- 1 small Broccoli Head

- 1 small bunch Fresh Basil

- 1 clove Garlic, finely chopped

- 3 Spring Onions, finely chopped

- 1 cup Pizza Cheese

- 3/4 cup Crème Fraiche

- Salt and Black Pepper, to taste

Steps

1. Add the flour and yeast into a food processor, and mix it together. Pour olive oil and tepid water slowly into the feeding tube of your food processor, as it blends. Keep processing until the dough comes together. Once it has, flour a clean surface in your kitchen and turn the dough out. Finish kneading it, and then shape the dough into a ball and place into a bowl covered with cling wrap, and let it rise for about 30 minutes. It should double in size.

2. Cook the broccoli florets in lightly salted water for about 3-4 minutes until they are al dente. Drain and

then rinse the broccoli thoroughly with cold water, and leave in the sink to thoroughly drain.

3. Clean your food processor bowl, and then add basil and garlic to be finely chopped. Once done, add the crème fraiche and pulse the food processor until you get a lovely green sauce. Season the sauce with salt and black pepper to your desired taste.

4. Preheat your Air Fryer to 428F (220C)

5. Divide the dough into 4 sections, and turn them out onto a lightly floured surface. Roll each piece of dough into a circle until the dough is about 2-3cm thick on the edges, and about 1-2cm thick in the middle.

6. Lightly grease the basket of your Air Fryer and place the pizza dough circles in the basket, two at a time (so two batches). Spread the basil sauce over the pizzas and top with broccoli and spring onions. Finish with a sprinkle of cheese.

7. Bake for 15 minutes in your Air Fryer until the crust is golden.

Notes

- Try using any combination of fresh herbs, such as rosemary, parsley, thyme or marjoram.

Salmon Patties

These patties taste excellent on their own, sitting over mashed potatoes, or served on a bun like a burger. They are full of fresh flavor and create an excellent nutritious meal.

Makes: 6-8 Patties

Ingredients

- 1 medium piece Salmon

- 3 large Russet Potatoes

- 1 handful Frozen Vegetable Medley

- 1 Egg

- 1 1/3 cup Panko Breadcrumbs

- 2 sprinkles Dill

- Chopped Parsley

- Salt and Black Pepper to taste

- Olive Oil Spray

Steps

1. Wash, peel, and chop the potatoes into small cubes. Boil a large pot of water, and boil the potato cubes for about 10 minutes. You only want them to be fork tender, not mushy. Drain the water, then replace the potatoes in the pot over low heat. Making sure you don't burn the potatoes, cook for about 2-3 minutes to let the remaining water evaporate. When they're done, mash the potatoes and pour them into a large, clean bowl to refrigerate until they're cool enough to handle.

2. Preheat the Air Fryer to 356F (180C). Once it's hot, grill your salmon for about 5 minutes. When it's done, use a fork to flake the salmon, and then set it aside.

3. Parboil your vegetables, either by cooking them in

water on the stove or steaming them in the microwave.

4. When they're cool enough to handle, take the mashed potatoes out of the fridge. In the bowl of potatoes, add flaked salmon, chopped parsley, parboiled vegetables, dill, salt, and pepper. Taste everything to make sure it is to your liking, if not, add some seasonings to achieve your desired flavor. When you have, add your egg and thoroughly mix all of the ingredients together.

5. Shape the mixture into 6-8 patties, and coat them with breadcrumbs. Spray some oil over the patties, ensuring to cover the breadcrumbs so they brown nicely.

6. Air Fry the patties for about 10-12 minutes on the grill pan.

7. Serve with any garnishing you like, such as mayo and lemon, with a side of salad.

Notes

- If you don't have fresh salmon available, you can use a can that has about 400g of flaked salmon instead. Just skip the steps where you cook and flake the salmon.

Spicy Tuna Roll

These spicy tuna rolls are a fun variation of the spicy tuna rolls that are served in sushi restaurants. Each bite-sized piece is crispy, rich in flavor, and lack the seaweed portion of sushi.

Makes: 4-6 Servings

Ingredients

- 150g Sashimi-Grade Tuna

- 2 Green Onions

- 1 teaspoon Sugar

- 1 teaspoon Sriracha Sauce

- 4 cups Cooked Sticky Rice

- 3 tablespoons Rice Vinegar

- Olive Oil Cooking Spray

Steps

1. Prepare your sushi rice to start by taking your cooked sticky rice and adding the vinegar and sugar, then mixing thoroughly.

2. Slice, then dice the tuna into small pieces.

3. Mix the tuna chunks with soy sauce and Sriracha Sauce to create your spicy tuna topping.

4. Take your rice and place it onto plastic wrap, then into a bamboo sheet.

5. Roll the bamboo sheet tightly, and squeeze to form your rice into a long even strip. Make sure it is tightly packed, to prevent it from falling apart during the cooking process.

6. Wet your knife and fingers so the rice doesn't stick, then cut your rice into nigiri chunks (about 1/2" to 1" pieces).

7. Place each rice chunk into the Air Fryer basket and Air Fry for 13 minutes at 392F (200C).

8. Once it's cooked, remove from the Air Fryer, and top with the Spicy Tuna.

9. Serve immediately.

Notes

- If you don't like tuna, you can swap the tuna out for salmon to create a spicy salmon roll! Just make sure to purchase sashimi-grade salmon.

Sticky BBQ Pork Strips

These pork strips are delicious on their own, or served over top of the salad, rice, or in a sandwich! They are a very versatile dish that can complement nearly any dish. Each piece is carefully cooked with a rich BBQ sauce flavoring.

Makes: 6-8 Servings

Ingredients

- 6 Pork Loin Chops

- 2 tablespoons Soy Sauce

- 2 tablespoons Honey

- 1 teaspoon Balsamic Vinegar

- 1/4 teaspoon Ground Ginger (or 1/2 teaspoon freshly grated ginger)

- 1 clove Garlic

- Fresh Ground Pepper to taste

Steps

1. Tenderize the pork chops with a meat tenderizer, then, season them with some ground fresh pepper.

2. In a bowl, make your marinade by mixing: balsamic vinegar, soy sauce, and honey. Add chopped garlic and ground ginger, and mix the ingredients well. Set the marinade aside for now.

3. Place the pork chops in a container large enough to marinate them, and then pour your marinade in. Mix them well to coat the chops well, and try and arrange

it so that each chop soaks well in the marinade. Leave it for 2 hours, or overnight if you have the time.

4. When you're ready to cook them, preheat your Air Fryer to 356F (180C).

5. Place your chops in the baking tray with some of the marinade juice and cook for about 5-8 minutes on each side. Make sure it is cooked thoroughly and turns golden brown.

6. Once it is cooked through, cut the meat into strips and serve over salad, rice, or mashed potatoes. Or, skip the cutting portion and serve as chops.

5 - Desserts

Apple Pie Pastries

Apple pie is a major favorite around here. These pastries resemble delicious little bite-sized apple pies. They are sweet, buttery, and make wonderful desserts.

Makes: 10 Apple Pie Pastries

Ingredients

- 3 medium Gala Apples, peeled and diced into tiny cubes

- 1 tablespoon Lemon Juice

- 2 teaspoons All-Purpose Flour

- 2 teaspoons Cinnamon

- 2 teaspoons Brown Sugar

- 1/2 teaspoon Nutmeg

- 1/2 teaspoon Ground Cloves (optional)

- 10 sheets of Filo Pastry

- 3/4 cup Butter, melted

Steps

1. If frozen, thaw Filo Pastries.

2. In a medium mixing bowl, combine lemon juice, flour, chopped apples, sugar, and spices.

3. Sanitize an area of the counter, and unroll all of the filo pastries onto it. Alternatively, you could unroll them onto a tea towel, or parchment paper.

4. Cover the pastries with a damp tea towel to prevent them from drying out. Make sure this towel stays damp the entire time.

5. Working with one Filo pastry at a time, lay it flat on parchment paper. Brush the pastry sparingly with melted butter.

6. Using a 1/3 cup scoop, place a single scoop of the filling in the center of the filo pastry sheet, leaving about two inches of space at the bottom. Fold the pastry similar to a burrito: first, fold the bottom up

over the filling, then fold the two sides in. Once the folds are tight, roll the rest of the pastry up, and brush lightly with melted butter. You can brush the pastry with a thin layer of melted butter throughout the folding process to keep it moist and help it stick together well.

7. Once you are done folding, brush the entire apple pie pastry, front and back, with melted butter. Sprinkle with brown sugar, if you want, or just leave it as is.

8. Preheat the Air Fryer to 320F (160C) for about 5 minutes, then bake the pastries two or three at a time, depending what will fit in the Air Fryer basket. Bake the pastries for 6-8 minutes, making sure they're evenly cooking about halfway through. Depending on the final size, cook time may vary so make sure you check in periodically to prevent overcooking or burning. They should look lightly golden, and the apple pieces should be soft when you insert a tooth pick in the center.

9. Allow the pastries to cool slightly before serving, to prevent burns. However, make sure to serve them be-

fore they're too cold, as they are best enjoyed warm.

10. These apple pie pastries can be served as is, or served with icing glass, whip cream, or a scoop of vanilla ice cream on the side.

Banana Split

Banana splits are a rich, sweet and fruity dessert. They can be enjoyed in a wide number of ways, with several options for toppings and flavor combinations. Here, we will enjoy fried bananas that have been coated with a crunchy bread crust, and topped with some delicious vanilla ice cream. This recipe also features a vegan option.

Makes: 8 Servings

Ingredients

- 3 tablespoons Butter (or Coconut Oil if you're vegan)

- 8 medium Bananas, ripe

- 2 large Eggs, lightly beaten

- 1/2 cup Corn Flour

- 3 tablespoons Cinnamon Sugar (or mix 1 tablespoon of Cinnamon + 2 tablespoons Sugar)

- 1 cup Panko Breadcrumbs

- Vanilla Ice Cream, for garnish

- Whip Cream, for garnish

Steps

1. Heat the butter (or coconut oil) in a pan over medium heat. Once melted, add the panko breadcrumbs. Stir the panko and butter for about 3-4 minutes, or until the breadcrumbs have acquired a light golden color. Remove the mixture from the heat and place in a medium-sized mixing bowl.

2. Preheat your Air Fryer to 280F (137C)

3. Peel your bananas, halve them and then coat them. To coat them, roll each piece of banana in corn flour, then dip into the eggs, and finally cover them with breadcrumbs. Place each banana half into your Air Fryer basket, side by side in a single layer. Once the

basket is full, dust the contents with cinnamon sugar.

4. Place the Air Fryer basket into the fryer and set the timer for 7 minutes. Once the timer is up, remove the basket, and shake it to remove any excess bread-crumbs from the bananas.

5. Serve each piece of banana warm with a scoop of vanilla ice cream and topped with whip cream, or whatever other garnish varieties you may desire.

Notes

- Inspiration for garnish: fruit jelly or jam, ice cream syrups, fresh fruit (or thawed from frozen, with the juice), flavored ice creams, crushed nuts, etc.

Chocolate Cake

What's a recipe book without a chocolate cake recipe? This delicious chocolate cake takes minutes to prepare, and can be cooked right in your Air Fryer! It is rich, sweet, and de-livers the full chocolatey flavor that we all know and love so much.

Makes: 1 (8") Round Cake

Ingredients

- 1 1/2 cup Brown Sugar

- 3/4 cup All-Purpose Flour

- 1/2 cup Cocoa Powder, unsweetened

- 1/2 cup Milk

- 1/2 cup Hot Water

- 1/4 cup Vegetable Oil

- 1 teaspoon of Vanilla Extract

- 3/4 teaspoon of Baking Powder

- 3/4 teaspoon of Baking Soda

- 1/2 teaspoon Salt

- 1 large Egg

Steps

1. Preheat your Air Fryer to 356F (180C)

2. Combine the following ingredients in a large bowl: flour, cocoa powder, sugar, baking soda, baking powder, and salt.

3. Once you have thoroughly combined the above ingredients, add milk, egg, oil, and vanilla extract. Whisk to combine the batter thoroughly.

4. Finally, add your hot water and gently stir to make sure it is thoroughly blended.

5. The batter will thin after you add the hot water, this is normal and desired.

6. Carefully pour the chocolate cake batter into a baking pan and cover the baking pan with foil and poke some holes in the foil for ventilation.

7. Place the baking pan in the Air Fryer basket, and adjust the temperature to 320F (160C). Air Bake the cake for 35 minutes. Remove the foil, then bake for an additional 10 minutes. The skewer should come out clean to signify the cake is done.

8. Allow the cake to thoroughly cool in the pan to prevent it from falling apart. It is a very moist and soft cake, so removing it too early could cause it to crumble.

9. Ice with your favorite icing.

Notes

- For added flavor, you can add a bit of instant coffee into the hot water.

Chocolate Chip Cookies

Chocolate chip cookies are a wonderful dessert. They can be made in large batches and eaten after dinner or added into packed lunches as a part of your daily snacks. These chocolate chip cookies are sweet, tasty, and so easy to make.

Makes: 9 Small Cookies, or 6 Large

Ingredients

- 2/3 cup Brown Sugar

- 1 1/2 cup Self-Rising Flour

- 1 cup Chocolate Chips

- 1 cup Butter

- 2 tablespoons Honey

- 1 tablespoon Milk

Steps

1. Preheat Air Fryer to 356F (180C)

2. In a large, clean mixing bowl, beat the butter until it is soft. Mix in the sugar, cream them together until the two are light and fluffy.

3. Once the two combine, stir in the honey and flour and mix thoroughly.

4. Add the chocolate to the bowl, and continue mixing. Finally, stir the milk in and mix thoroughly.

5. Once the dough is thoroughly combined, spoon it into the air fryer on a greased baking sheet.

6. Bake the cookies for 6 minutes. Reduce the temperat-

ure to 320F (160C), and bake for an extra 2 minutes so they are thoroughly cooked in the middle.

7. Serve warm!

Homemade Cinnamon Donuts

These homemade donuts take less than 3 minutes to prepare and cook in no time at all. They use Jumbo Flaky Biscuits and a few extra ingredients. Though they are not made entirely from scratch, they could definitely pass for it, as they are so delicious!

Makes: 24-26 Donuts

Ingredients

- Jumbo Flaky Biscuits (the premade kind in a cardboard tube that you bake at home. Any brand will suffice)

- 1/2 cup Sugar

- 1 tablespoon Cinnamon

- Cooking Oil Spray

Steps

1. Preheat your Air Fryer to 356F (180C)

2. Remove the biscuits from the cardboard tube, and cut each one into quarters.

3. Spray the Air Fryer basket with cooking oil spray and toss in the biscuit quarters. Spray the biscuits with cooking oil spray as well.

4. Cook the biscuits for the recommended time on the box (usually around 7-12 minutes)

5. When they're done, remove them from the basket, and place them in a medium mixing bowl. Combine the sugar and cinnamon in a separate container and then pour them in over the donuts. Toss them to evenly coat them, and then serve immediately. Alternative, store them in an air tight container in the fridge for up to 3 days.

Marble Cake

This marble cake is moist, sweet, and looks beautiful. It

tastes wonderful, whether it has been covered in icing or with a sugary sweet glaze.

Ingredients

- 2/3 cup Butter, melted

- 3/4 cup Sugar

- 3 large Eggs

- 1 tablespoon Cocoa Powder

- 1 cup Self-Rising Flour, sieved

- 1/2 teaspoon Lemon Juice

Steps

1. Preheat Air Fryer to 356F (180C). Grease a 5" round pan, and set it inside of the Fryer Basket (but not in the Air Fryer)

2. Using 1/3 of the total butter, melt it in a bowl and then add the cocoa powder. Mix the two until they become a smooth paste, and then set aside.

3. Take the remaining melted butter and whisk it until it is pale in color.

4. Whisk the eggs in a cup, then pour into the butter mixture. Alternating with the flour, then stir until the batter is smooth.

5. Finally, add the lemon juice to the batter and blend well.

6. Preheat the empty pan for about 1 minute. Take it back out.

7. Slowly pour the batter into the pan, alternating with the cocoa mixture. Using a knife, create a swirl between the two.

8. Bake the cake for about 15-17 minutes, then let the cake cool in the pan. Then remove the cake to let it complete the cooling process.

Red Velvet Cupcakes

These scrumptious red velvet cupcakes are wonderful treats. They are excellent for desserts and wonderful for parties. This recipe features a delicious homemade butter-cream frosting, but also pairs well with a cream cheese frosting.

Makes: 4-6 Cupcakes

Ingredients

- 3 Eggs, beaten

- 2 cups Refined Flour

- 1 cup Cream Cheese

- 1 cup Frosting Hard Butter

- 3/4 cup Icing Sugar

- 3/4 cup Icing Sugar

- 3/4 cup Peanut Butter

- 1/4 cup Strawberry Sauce (optional)

- 2 teaspoons Beet Powder

- 1 teaspoon Cocoa Powder

- 1 teaspoon Vanilla Essence

- Garnish

- 1 Strawberry (for each cupcake)

- Grated Chocolate

Steps

1. Preheat your Air Fryer to 356F (180C)

2. Take a medium bowl and combine the following: eggs, icing sugar, creamy peanut butter, cocoa powder, beet powder, and refined flour. Beat with an electric mixer to blend thoroughly.

3. Pour the batter into silicon cupcake molds.

4. Reduce the temperature of the Air Fryer to 338F (170C) and bake the cupcakes for 10-12 minutes.

5. When the cupcakes are done baking, remove them from the Air Fryer and let them cool for 15 minutes or so.

6. In a clean bowl, beat together: hard butter, icing sugar, and vanilla with the electric mixer.

7. Let the cupcakes cool, then top them with your homemade icing, and garnish with a strawberry and some grated chocolate.

6 - Snacks

Apple Pie Fries

These sweet fries are a wonderful snack. They are comprised of a few different store-bought ingredients, and some stuff you'll have in your pantry. Apple pie fries taste phenomenal when dipped in caramel sauce.

Makes: 2-4 Servings

Ingredients

- 1 (2 piece) package Refrigerated Pie Crust

- 1 (10oz) can Apple Pie Filling

- 1/4 cup Sugar

- 1 teaspoon Cinnamon

- 1/4 teaspoon Nutmeg

- 1 Egg

- Sparkling Sugar

- Olive Oil Spray

- Caramel Dip (optional)

Steps

1. Let your crusts heat up to room temperature on the counter, for about 15 minutes.

2. Preheat your Air Fryer to 350F (177C)

3. Lightly dust your work area with flour and roll out the crusts a bit.

4. Pulse the pie filling in a food processor until it is in smaller pieces.

5. Spread the apple pie filling over top of 1 of the crusts, leaving roughly 1/8" uncovered at the edges, and top with the 2nd crust.

6. Cut your apple pie sandwich into 1/2" strips, and then shorten your strips into the length of fries.

7. In a clean bowl, beat an egg until it is well-blended. In a separate clean bowl, combine sugar, cinnamon, and nutmeg until it is thoroughly mixed.

8. Brush the tops of the fries with the beaten egg, then gently sprinkle the sugar mixture over top of them.

9. Sprinkle sparkling sugar over the tops, and then transfer the fries into a greased Air Fry basket.

10. Bake the apple fries for 15-20 minutes. The fries should be golden brown and crispy on the outside.

Banana Chips

Banana chips are a delicious, healthy snack that can be enjoyed anytime. They are excellent for packed lunches or snacking between meals. You can even top them with things such as almond butter and shaved coconut to make an even healthier snack!

Makes: 30-40+ Chips, Depending on Thickness

Ingredients

- 3-4 Bananas, peeled

- 1/2 teaspoon Turmeric Powder

- 1/2 teaspoon Chaat Masala

- 1 teaspoon Salt

- 1 teaspoon Oil

Steps

1. In a small bowl, mix together turmeric powder, and salt, then add some water until it has a soupy consistency. Cut your banana slices in this mixture, as it will prevent the bananas from turning black, and maintain a nice yellow color. You will want your bananas to soak in this mixture for about 5-10 minutes before proceeding to the next step.

2. Drain the water, and pat your bananas dry. Now, apply a little oil on the chips to prevent them from sticking in your Air Fryer.

3. Preheat your fryer to 180 degrees, and give it about 5 minutes to heat up. Once warm, add the chips and air fry them for about 15 minutes. Sprinkle them with salt and chaat masala.

4. To preserve these, store them in an airtight jar or serve immediately.

Notes

Try your chips with these different toppings:

- Almond Butter and Coconut Shavings

- Peanut Butter and Walnuts

- Cream Cheese and Raisins

Or you can try them with these different dips:

- Hummus

- Roasted Garlic Cream Cheese Dip

- Dill Pickle Cream Cheese Dip

Corn Tortilla Chips

These homemade tortilla chips taste delicious dipped in salsa or turned into a nacho chip dish. They are a wonderful snack, and work well for game night.

Makes: 4-6 Servings

Ingredients

- 8 medium to large Corn Tortillas

- 1 tablespoon Olive Oil

- Salt, to taste

Steps

1. Preheat your Air Fryer to 200C (392F)

2. Brush both sides of the corn tortillas with olive oil.

3. Using a sharp knife, cut the tortillas into triangles like a pizza.

4. Place half of the tortilla triangles into the wire basket and Air Fry for 3 minutes. Repeat this process for the second batch.

5. Sprinkle the chips with salt, and serve.

Notes

You can add some flavor to these chips by mixing the tablespoon of olive oil in a bowl with some fresh chopped herbs such as chives or parsley.

Crispy Kale Chips

Kale chips are a crispy alternative to potato chips and much healthier as well. These chips are made in your Air Fryer and can be seasoned to a limitless number of tastes. Here, we will make them with soya sauce.

Makes: 2-4 Servings

Ingredients

- 1 tablespoon Olive Oil

- 1 teaspoon Soya Sauce

- 1 medium Head of Kale

Steps

1. Preheat the Air Fryer to 200C (392F)

2. Thoroughly rinse and clean your kale, then shake off the excess water and let it dry for a couple of minutes. Once dry, remove the center stem and tear the kale up into 1 1/2" pieces.

3. In a medium bowl, toss the kale with soya sauce and olive oil.

4. Place the kale in the Air Fryer basket and cook for 2-3 minutes, tossing basket half way through.

Mashed Potato "Tater Tots"

Tater tots are a quick and easy snack to make. They also pair deliciously with a breakfast of eggs and bacon. They are filling and can be used with any number of dipping sauces.

Makes: 1-2 Servings

Ingredients

- 1 Red Potato

- 1 teaspoon Onion, minced

- 1 teaspoon Olive Oil

- Salt and Pepper to taste

Steps

1. Preheat the Air Fryer to 379F (192C)

2. Clean and peel the potato, then cook it in the microwave for about 1-2 minutes so it's al dente.

3. In a medium bowl, mash the potato with oil, onion, salt and pepper until it is well mashed. When you've completed this, form the mash into tater tots (small cylinders).

4. Put the tater tots in the Air Fryer basket, and cook for 7-8 minutes. Toss the basket, and then cook them for another 5 minutes. When they're golden brown and cooked through, they're done.

5. Serve with your sauce of choice or as a side for a meal.

Onion Chips

These crispy onion chips are a delicious snack. They are healthy, crunchy, and taste great. This recipe features a wonderful horseradish aioli that you can make to dip the onion chips in.

Makes: 4 Servings

Ingredients

- 1 large Vidalia Onion

- 1 1/2 cup Cornmeal

- 1 1/4 cup Buttermilk

- 1 teaspoon Salt

- 1 teaspoon Black Pepper

- Horseradish Aioli

- 1/2 cup Mayo

- 2 tablespoons Horseradish Cream

- Juice of 1/2 Lemon

- Salt & Pepper to taste

Steps

1. Preheat your Air Fryer to 350F (177C)

2. Peel the onion, and slice it thinly. If you're using a

mandolin slicer, set it between 1/8" and 1/4".

3. In a large milk, pour in your buttermilk, then add the onion slices. While adding them, carefully separate the rings so the onion resembles strings.

4. In a wide dish shallow dish, mix together the salt, pepper, and cornmeal.

5. Take the onions, shake the excess buttermilk off, and then toss them in the cornmeal to coat them evenly. Then place them in the Air Fryer basket.

6. Cook the onions for about 3-5 minutes until they're crispy and golden. Air Fry in batches to prevent overcrowding the basket.

7. While the onions cook, mix together the following ingredients to make horseradish aioli: mayo, horseradish cream, juice of 1/2 lemon, salt & pepper to taste. Serve this aioli with the onion strings.

Potato Chips

Potato chips are a wonderfully crispy, salty snack. Now, you don't have to buy your chips at the store. You can make them right in your own home, using you Air Fryer!

Ingredients

- 2 medium Russet Potatoes

- 1/2 tablespoon Extra Virgin Olive Oil

- Salt to taste

Steps

1. Scrub the potatoes clean and, if you want to, peel them before you thinly slice them. This can easily be done using a mandolin or the long side on a food grater.

2. In a large bowl, soak the potato slices in cold water for about 15 minutes. Change the water, give the slices a good toss, and soak for another 15 minutes.

3. Spread the potato slices out on paper towels or a clean tea towel, then blot to dry.

4. Return the slices to the bowl, and mix them with ex-

tra virgin olive oil, and a little salt.

5. Preheat the Air Fryer to 392F (200C) for about 5 minutes, and cook for approximately 22 minutes or until crispy.

6. Empty the chips into a bowl, add extra salt, and any other seasonings you desire.

Roasted Chickpeas

Roasted chickpeas are as tasty as they look. Due to the nature of them, they qualify as vegan snacks as well. They are salty (or sweet, depending on your seasoning mix) and crunchy, and an excellent snack.

Makes: 2-4 Servings

Ingredients

- 1 (16oz) can Chickpeas, rinsed and drained

- 1-2 tablespoons Mixed Seasonings

- 1/2 tablespoon Olive Oil

Steps

1. Preheat the Air Fryer to 356F (180C)

2. Drain the can of chickpeas and rinse them thoroughly

3. In a medium bowl, toss the chickpeas with olive oil and your seasonings of choice. Make sure they are evenly coated.

4. Place the chickpeas in your Air Fryer basket and cook for about 8-10 minutes.

7 - Conclusion

Thank you again for downloading this Air Fryer Cookbook!

I hope this book was able to help you get the most out of your Air Fryer! The healthy recipes are delicious, simple, and help you put your Air Fryer to good use.

The next step is to pick your favorite recipes, pick up the required ingredients and get cooking.

Thank You

As we reach the end of this book, I want to say thanks for reading this book.

I want to get this information out to as many people as possible. If you found this book helpful, I would greatly appreciate you leaving me a review on Amazon here. This helps others find the book as well.

I love hearing from readers so please get in touch via E-mail: cabpublishing1@gmail.com[1]

---

[1]mailto:cabpublishing1@gmail.com

Disclaimer

This document is geared towards providing exact and reliable information in regards to the topic and issue covered. The publication is sold with the idea that the publisher is not required to render accounting, officially permitted, or otherwise, qualified services. If advice is necessary, legal or professional, a practiced individual in the profession should be ordered.

This information is not presented by a medical practicioner and is for educational and informational purposes only. The content is not intended as a substitute for professional medical advice, diagnosis, or treatment. Always seek the advice of your physician or other qualified health care provider with any questions you may have regarding a medical condition. Never disregard professional medical advice or delay in seeking it because of something you have read.

The information provided herein is stated to be truthful and consistent, in that any liability, in terms of inattention or otherwise, by any usage or abuse of any policies, processes, or directions contained within is the solitary and utter responsibility of the recipient reader. Under no circumstances will any legal responsibility or blame be held against the